On the Way to Work

Also by Ian Davidson

Partly in Riga (Shearsman, 2010)
As if Only (Shearsman, 2007)
At a Stretch (Shearsman, 2004)
Harsh (Spectacular Diseases, 2003)

Poetry Pamphlets

Gateshead and Back: Vol. 2 of the Tyne and Wear Poems
        (London: Crater, 2017)
In Agitation (Newton le Willows: KFS, 2014)
The Tyne and Wear Poems (Newcastle: Red Squirrel Press, 2014)
Into Thick Hair (Dublin: Wild Honey Press, 2010)
Familiarity Breeds (Norwich: Oystercatcher Press, 2008)
Dark Wires (with Zoe Skoulding) (Sheffield: West House Books, 2007)
No Way Back (Sheffield: West House Books, 2004)
Human Remains and Sudden Movements
        (Sheffield: West House Books, 2003)
Wipe Out (Cheltenham: Short Run, 1995)
Human to Begin With (Cambridge: Poetical Histories, 1991)
The Patrick Poems (London: Amra Imprint, 1991)
No Passage Landward (Hebden Bridge: Open Township, 1989)
It Is Now as It Was Then (with John Muckle) (London: Actual Size, 1983)

On the Way to Work

Ian Davidson

Shearsman Books

First published in the United Kingdom in 2017 by
Shearsman Books
50 Westons Hill Drive
Emersons Green
BRISTOL
BS16 7DF

Shearsman Books Ltd Registered Office
30–31 St. James Place, Mangotsfield, Bristol BS16 9JB
(this address not for correspondence)

www.shearsman.com

ISBN 978-1-84861-562-5

Contents

Vol. 3

of

The Tyne and Wear Poems

1. LSD

1.
Beyond the
bus shelter
and on the
way to work
I was feeling
finite from
the truths
that make me
as the river
ran or the
money kept
flowing

2.
I was on my
way to work
when this void
opened up see
and I looked
into it and then
it was all
around me
so I called out
to it hey void
what can we
do about it
well you

called me void
it answered and
that's something

3.
on the way to
work I wanted
LSD and the
experience of
really seeing

myself as I
truly am

on the way
to work I
admired my
reflection

on the way to
work it had
been Purim
and the children
wore disguises
and the fathers
were drunk

on the way to
work the urge
for LSD is

almost unbearable
like a fat cigarette
on a swollen lip
the beating
vanes of a
pursuit heli-
copter so I
chewed coca
to keep the
weight from my
legs I count the
blasts from deep
down where the
devil lives and
smokes cigarettes
and drinks the
blood of lamas
and the thin grey
mud from the
wet clay coats
everything I shrug
myself into an
overall thick with
oil feeling the
cold concrete
and devil far
below urging
me down to
where the silver
falls like dust

4.

walking home from
work under azure
blue the avenues
holding light at
their termination I
don't regret she
said one single
minute she said
not a single minute

2. Eternity rings

Completed works are a narcotic

there was too
much space and
not enough to
get my head
around or like
a turban
wound or the
time it took
say finitude or
thereabouts
not the shift-
ing forms to
eternity or the
fin of my
encircling fish
that go round
and round and
live in my room and
see me when
I sleep

3. Pigeons come and go

From a train window
a beaten man stands
amongst the pigeon lofts
little more than sheds
along the track as
pigeons circle
with intent around
his pigeon post.

A carrier of bad
news the pigeon
comes home to
roost some people
are beaten up over
and over some
people are
inclined to
stay put others

are after utopia
or the bit when
the poem
flutters to the ground
its syllables
vulnerable its
shame the
frayed feathers
beaten flat.

Some pigeons
never come home
to roost some
pigeons are
stoolies some
men only stand
and wait their
beaten faces their
feathered edge.

4. Void again

you called me void you
said you called me
heaven under a
starry sky hello he
said the sound
became a thin
blue stream
the birds were in flocks
the fields rectangles
that cannot
contain themselves

5. Prisons

for lara pearson

A prison is and surround-
ed by silence and a parched
concrete moat. No voices clear
the walls from open throats to

reach the scrub woods or the em-
pty sky. I thought the heavens
might have sucked out the bad things
to where the passing express

trains easily released en-
ergy. But the only es-
caping sound is from kennels
whose inmates are dogs that howl

out their immobility.
I half expected their a-
ppearance, these voices through the
open top like a lanced boil

past remote cameras swi-
velling on their poles it is
forbidden to reverse a
vehicle up to the pri-

son walls without supervisi-
on it was clear we were un-
der surveillance that we see
ourselves coming closer a-

long ways that were medie-
val, the smooth surface of the
river the lush valley where
fish jump while in the free world,

the hot back alleys and crumb-
ling yards of home, where there is
little exercise to be
had, the crack of fired up en-

gines, the ever present po-
lice on soft rubber across
the cobbles people shouting
at the tops of their voices

in these places on the out-
side of the smooth surfaces
of prison that resist the
friction of guilty or not

guilty in indifference
to any ambivalence be-
tween what things might mean in the
enactment of due process.

And outside prison, where there
is purchase, even on soft
brick, spalled. Prisons, you just
come across them and their sheer

walls, razor wire knitted in
intricate shapes. I go a-
round a prison cautiously,
whatever its category.

6. A Bridge Poem

It was an old
car and
near the end of its
life but the
thing we talked
about was remi-
niscent of that
other thing, you
know that thing
we never talk
about you know

It was a
long bridge
across the Hum-
ber or the
Tyne or the
Menai Strait
but that's
bridges for you
we can cross
on foot or behind
the wheel for
hours on end

Bridges
might sway

in a stiff wind an
earthquake is
undetectable in
a car on a
bridge these
are insulatory
factors, rubber
mainly, and wire
and then in

The dead centre
of the bridge I
turn and ask you
to stop and
think and
look both back
and forward and
ask yourself I
like the dead

Centre of a bridge
with its bouquets
of flowers
but sometimes I
just drive across
in my old car
and avoid the
lightning strikes
or the sudden
drops or the river
down below

7. Spirit of Blyth

Down the eastern side from
north Blyth around the bend
in the river to the biomass
shipped in past the staiths
workers have always been
on the move queuing for

their chips, for parking spaces
outside of the yellow lines
that restrict rest. I think these things
between night and day where
the labour of orthodoxy

grinds on through the morning
news and forced to the surface
as the day dawns. I can't
believe mumsnet has been
hacked or anyone is surprised
that Facebook is no longer cool

or depths that cannot be plumbed.
It is only later in the day
of course that the surface is
probed by intelligence
until there is little
left to kick at no straight
forward explosion of fact.

An ied will only send things a
little off course the gossamer
air and heavy scent of jasmine
only part of a summer walk the
rest is pacing and heavy tread.

8. Voices

Talking is a reverse
process sometimes
words are like picks
and shovels mining

a mind's rich seams
its levels propped.
Voices are like tuned
wires sometimes

like a stringed
instrument.
Voices get rusty
sometimes with

misuse or burnt out.
Voices are the things
left behind and
a future forecast,

talking is a mirror
sometimes in which
we hear ourselves
and as I was saying.

9. Coming and Going

1.
I wanted to
bring this up
like dry crying
when I arrive
like tears
when I leave so
I cry or don't
cry whatever
comes to hand
but then some
others came and
took whatever
and then some
others said
that was wrong
that those others
took the things
so fascism

2.
The direction of
travel is no
way back and
on the way to
work where
no Engarlish

is spoken and
in London town
where the
queen lives the
lights are out
in London
town the lights
are out in
County Durham
where agents
from out of town
knock down
whole streets

3.
between cup
and lip over
broken glass
through gritted
teeth and
clenched fists
past barbed
speech or
clenched jaw
over broken
glass on bended
knees or shaken
like a rag doll
like a crash test
through swollen

lips I have
overheard too
much for
my own good

4.
the sun goes
in and out its
hourly rate
from sea to
shining centre
where the folding
money is
geology follows
the folds
in the hills
in low cloud
things glisten
sheep make
their mark
listen it is
a Friday and
the sea at the
valley's end
is a bikini

5.
speak to me
shingle of the
beach slap

me curling
water that makes
a wave spirits
rising like the
surface seabirds
disappearing
weaving home
from work
so miss me
heart beat
rattle my
throat the dry
sound that
powdered blood
makes

10. The Underpass

On the way to work the
underpass gave me the
V sign hey underpass
with your concrete V.

On the way to
work walking over
potential sink holes
the road showed

its foundations on the
way to work, over and
over, wearing away
until my voice breaks

with the length of the
sentence and the un
even surface of the
road and the ups

and downs the
blank even tone of
corporate structures
its cushioned blows.

The dancing boy forgot
himself temporarily
down the tunnels in
his head falling into

himself, the words
were like picks and
shovels his mind like
the trench in the road

mined for the
occasional cable or
network connection
my fingers into sockets

my trembling hands
my head crumbling
concrete that makes
the underpass where

reinforcing is beginning
to rust or these dark wires
long forgotten cables
anachronistic electronics

system obsolete the
fading pulse the beating
heart on the way to work
over and over.

Lightning Source UK Ltd.
Milton Keynes UK
UKOW05f1228090617

303026UK00002BA/146/P